The Complete Guide to Remote Online Notarization

How New Laws, Technologies, and Consumer Demands are Reshaping the Notarial Act and the Future of Trust in the Digital Age.

THE COMPLETE GUIDE TO REMOTE ONLINE NOTARIZATION

Copyright © 2019 by Notarize, Inc.

Printed in the United States. All rights reserved. No part of this book may be reproduced or used in any manner without written permission of the copyright owner except in the case of brief quotations embodied in critical articles and reviews.

2nd edition

Designed by Amy Ahrens

ISBN (9781796910858)

Published by Notarize, Inc. notarize.com

Millions of transactions will soon be conducted online.

This book is dedicated to those who are building the future of the trust economy, supporting life's most important moments around the world.

About the Authors

ANDREW MACDOUGALL

Andrew MacDougall is the Editor and Content Strategist at Notarize - the most trusted platform for signing and notarizing documents online - where he writes about the intersection of technology, accessibility, and digital trust.

Before joining Notarize, Andrew led communication efforts on behalf of the U.S. Department of Transportation and reported for The Boston Globe. He earned his B.A. in Journalism from Northeastern University.

MICHAEL CHODOS

Michael Chodos is the Senior Vice President and General Counsel at Notarize, as well as a Senior Fellow at Georgetown University's Beeck Center for Social Impact and Innovation.

Michael previously served as the head of the Office of Entrepreneurial Development in the U.S. Small Business Administration under President Barack Obama. He also served the Administration as the SBA's Deputy General Counsel. He earned his J.D. from Stanford University Law School.

Table of Contents

EXECUTIVE SUMMARY 1

CHAPTER 1 4
Technology and the Notary Public

CHAPTER 2 8
Remote Online Notarization, Explained

CHAPTER 3 11
Benefits of RON

CHAPTER 4 21
Laws and Recognition

CHAPTER 5 31
State of RON

CHAPTER 6 39
Milestones and Model Legislation

CONCLUSION 49
FAQS... 51
KEY TERMS 54
BIBLIOGRAPHY................................ 56

Executive Summary

Those of us old enough to remember dial-up Internet probably didn't consider it transformative at the time, but the loud, grating sounds of the early Internet brought the world to our fingertips. As technology evolves, it empowers society to improve those products and processes that it has relied on for hundreds of years.

The notarial act is no exception.

There are over 4.5 million notaries in the United States - public servants appointed by their states to ensure the authenticity and integrity of the document signing process. Innovation has long overlooked the notarial process.

But its time for transformation has finally come.

For centuries, the only way a notary could do their job was in person. You would take your notarial needs to a bank, title company, or small business service center with confidence, but many of these places no longer staff notaries or refuse to handle certain documents. You could scour Yelp or the Yellow Pages for hours without finding a definitive answer.

Today, your nearest notary is likely in your pocket.

Thanks to remote online notarization (RON), you can notarize a document from anywhere in the world, using your computer or mobile device. Remote online notarization was first brought to Americans across the globe by a 2011 Virginia law, which relies on secure audio and video feeds to connect signers with commissioned electronic notaries. Since its introduction, tens of thousands of transactions have been completed using RON technologies.

Through October 2019, 21 states have followed Virginia's lead by enacting laws allowing their notaries to use RON, while nearly every other state has explored its benefits.

Traditional, paper-based notarization is a blocker for everyday people and businesses. Technology can now unblock this workflow, saving time and money with a safer and more secure solution than what currently exists.

In one survey, 65% of real estate professionals said that they expect to adopt RON and secure collaboration and

communication portals by the end of 2019.[1] "Streamlining time-consuming processes, as well as delivering an improved consumer experience, is top of mind for real estate professionals," wrote Mark Fleming, chief economist at First American, in the November 2018 Real Estate Sentiment Index. "Fintech is here to stay."

This book will explain RON and its impact, its use cases, why it's more secure and accessible than the traditional notarial processes, and how it's forever transforming some of the largest sectors of the American economy.

---

[1] Fleming, Mark. "Will Fintech Adoption Among Real Estate Professionals Accelerate in 2019?" *First American*, 27 Nov. 2018, blog. firstam.com/economics/will-fintech-adoption-among-real-estate-professionals-accelerate-in-2019.

CHAPTER 1

Technology and the Notary Public

In our relatively anonymous but interconnected world, society demands a system that enforces and reinforces integrity, honesty, and trust. Having an impartial witness verify the authenticity of a transaction assures its integrity and is an equally powerful deterrent to fraud.

A notary seal is the original "Seal of Approval." It confirms that an objective third party verified the signer's identity, that the signer understood the contents of their documents, and that the signer signed those documents willingly.

The notary public originated in Angient Egypt, where scribes would record personal letters, tax records, and official proclamations. Today, notaries continue to serve a vital public service by empowering life's most important moments.

The Ever-Changing Landscape

The basic elements of a valid notarization have been the same for centuries: A signer appears before a notary. The notary then confirms the signer's identity, that they understand what they are signing, and that they are doing so willingly. Though the process remains the same, notarial tools have changed as society has modernized.

NOTARY TOOLS AND THEIR EVOLUTION

For hundreds of years, a notary stamped the document with a wax seal and signed it with a feather quill. Technology has introduced new tools into the signing process, but these tools haven't always been welcomed. The ball-point pen was initially viewed as a "made to order" tool for forgers, according to two members of the American Society of Questioned Document Examiners (ASQDE).[2,3]

2 *The American Society of Questioned Document Examiners.* www.asqde.org/.

3 Stein, Elbridge W., et al. "Ball-Point Pens: Use for Signing Legal Documents Considered." *American Bar Association Journal*, vol. 34, no. 5, 1948, pp. 373–378.

"The main objects in writing a signature in an individual way are to make distinctive and difficult to forge successfully. Both of these objects tend to be defeated by the use of a ball-point pen. The only individuality that can be put into a signature with this kind of a pen is the mere forms of the letter, and these are the easiest parts of a signature for a forger to imitate."

GOVERNMENT-ISSUED IDS

Identity confirmation tools have also evolved. Until the mid-20th century, there were only two ways for a notary to identify a signer: either the notary personally knew the signer, or the notary and signer knew a mutual party who could serve as a "credible witness" and identify the signer.

The widespread adoption of government-issued IDs in the 1940s vastly expanded access to notarizations as people could now be identified absent personal knowledge or a credible witness. The state and federal government became the third party. If the face on the card matched the face in front of the notary, the person was who they claim to be.

But just as notarial tools evolve, so does the potential for fraud. As technology strengthens accuracy, people look for new ways to cheat the system. The notarial act is not exempt.

TECHNOLOGY AND THE DIGITAL NOTARY

Throughout the 20th century, fraudsters developed increasingly sophisticated ways to forge signatures and fabricate forms of identification. This presents enormous challenges for traditional, paper-based notarizations, which lack digital tools that are better at catching fraud.

Incorporating technology into the notarial act ensures that a notary can properly authenticate a transaction. Modern tools that validate identity online, such as credential analysis and knowledge-based authentication, are mature and readily available, and applying a secure e-signature with thorough audit trails of the entire process are now commonplace.

Remote notarization platforms provide notaries with these powerful tools, empowering them to continue to perform their traditional function in a way that remains trustworthy and reliable in the Digital Age.

CHAPTER 2

Remote Online Notarization, Explained

People have long traveled to their local bank, title company, or small business service center to get their documents notarized, but locating a notary is becoming increasingly difficult. Many of these places no longer staff notaries or refuse to handle certain documents. You could scour the Internet for hours without finding the help you need.

Remote online notarization allows documents to be notarized in electronic form with the signer signing with an electronic signature and appearing before a commissioned electronic notary online via audio-video technology.

This allows anyone with an Internet connection to get

documents signed and notarized online.

You no longer have to schedule an in-person notary visit or negotiate an amicable time and place to meet a mobile notary. You can now connect with a notary using your laptop, tablet, or smartphone through third-party providers.

Remote online notarization should not be confused with face-to-face electronic notarization, where documents are similarly notarized in electronic form and with an electronic signature - usually by a notary who brings a laptop to the signing meeting. However, these notarizations are conducted in the physical presence of a notary public, meaning you must still schedule a time and place to meet with a notary or mobile notary.

Notarizing documents online is still in its early days, and so is the terminology surrounding it. Some people talk broadly about "electronic notarization" and, in doing so, include or exclude "remote online notarization." Others use the terms interchangeably. It's important to understand their unique differences to effectively communicate and avoid confusion.

Virginia Adopts RON

Through 2010, all digital enhancements to the notarial act were focused on face-to-face electronic notarization. Documents could be notarized in electronic form with an electronic signature, though the notarization still needed to occur in the physical presence of a notary.

This all changed in 2011 when Governor Bob McDonnell of Virginia signed House Bill 2318/Senate Bill 827 into law. The bill was the first in the country to allow commissioned Virginia electronic notaries to notarize documents online via audio-video technology.

The law was grounded in long-time audio-video appearance experience from court proceedings along with well-developed, heightened online identity validation techniques widely used across the federal sector. Coupled with interstate recognition practices, House Bill 2318/Senate Bill 827 gave all Americans a legal avenue to get their documents notarized from anywhere and at any time.

The bill went into effect in 2012 with the implementation of Virginia Code Section 47.1.[4]

---

4 "Title 47.1. Notaries and Out-of-State Commissioners." *Virginia's Legislative Information System*, law.lis.virginia.gov/vacode/title47.1/.

In 2013, Virginia released the Electronic Notarization Assurance Standard[5] to help ensure worldwide recognition and acceptance of documents notarized by Virginia electronic notaries.

Virginia flipped the notary world on its head. It changed the conversation about what technology could accomplish and the business processes tied to some of America's most important economic sectors.

---

5   The Virginia Electronic Notarization Assurance Standard. *Secretary of the Commonwealth of Virginia*, 21 Jan. 2013, www.commonwealth.virginia.gov/media/governorvirginiagov/secretary-of-the-commonwealth/pdf/VAe-NotarizationStandard2013Version10.pdf.

CHAPTER 3

Benefits of RON

Validating someone's identity is a pillar of the notarial act, and fundamental in a transaction where you need to trust the person on the other end. Vendors that stand out in the RON space prioritize security and invest in cutting-edge identity verification and authentication technologies that make the process easier and more certain.

Here's how they do it.

1. Fraud Prevention Through Modern Securities

Identity proofing is complicated. While forgery does occur, the most common issue for notaries is human error. Notaries are human beings, and mistakes happen from time to time.

State- and government-issued proofs of identification capture a person at a specific moment in time. Maybe it was before they had glasses, or when they had a beard and a couple extra pounds. Licenses and passports don't account for time, and so it's often difficult to ensure the person before you is the person in the photo from several years ago.

Research shows that ID verification is difficult even with years of practice.[6] A 2014 survey conducted by the National Notary Association (NNA)[7] found that more than 32% of the 2,900 participants failed to catch imposters in an ID-matching quiz. The same group claimed people who matched their IDs were imposters 31% of the time.[8]

---

6   Papesh, Megan H. "Photo ID verification remains challenging despite years of practice" *Cognitive Research: Principles and Implications*, vol. 3 19. 27 Jun. 2018.

7   *National Notary Association*, www.nationalnotary.org/.

8   Lewis, Michael. "The Notary Challenge: Matching Faces To ID Harder Than You Think." *National Notary Association*, Sept. 2014, www.nationalnotary.org/notary-bulletin/blog/2014/09/matching-faces-to-id-harder.

A follow-up survey from the NNA and Louisiana State University in 2015 found that a pool of 1,150 notaries could only identify imposters 72% of the time.[9]

Today's notaries need access to additional online, database-driven identity verification tools that help them verify the identity of signers appearing before them.

In the future, these tools may well include biometric verifiers, "smart" cards with encoded digital identity information, and other tools. Fundamental to this process will be the use of multiple factors of identity verification which will ensure that identity verification is strong while making it harder to commit fraud.

CREDENTIALS CAPTURED AND ANALYZED INSTANTLY

Before photo IDs, a person's identity could only be verified by someone they knew or by someone who knew the notary. Photo IDs brought about an enhanced form of verification. Years later, as IDs became easier to forge, it became harder to accurately identify the validity of a person's credentials.

---

9   Lewis, Michael. "Notaries Post Mixed Results In Face-Matching Research Survey." *National Notary Association*, 12 Nov. 2015, www.nationalnotary.org/notary-bulletin/blog/2015/11/face-matching-research-results.

Think about all those movie scenes where someone gets into a bar with their fake ID. Now, people are using these fake IDs to forge signatures on deeds or powers of attorney.

When it comes to protecting identity in an age of technology, we need extra layers that ensure the person on the other end of a transaction is, in fact, who they say they are.

With RON, identity proofing begins with credential analysis. For in-person notarizations, this requires the notary to review a state- or government-issued photo ID or passport and determine if the person sitting in front of them matches the ID. When doing this remotely, an additional layer of analysis is added, running the ID through software-based processes to make sure it isn't fake, and that it's valid.

SECURITY QUESTIONS TAILORED TO YOU

It's becoming easier to steal, replicate, or duplicate forms of ID, but it's hard to steal knowledge and personal experience.

Knowledge-Based Authentication (KBA) is a popular security feature that helps identify and prevent fraud. Most people are familiar with "static" KBA questions from setting up online accounts, but there is a more nuanced "dynamic" KBA that is becoming increasingly common and vitally important to identity verification.

With static KBA, new users answer a series of fixed questions that pertain to their personal experiences: "What street did you grow up on?" "What was the name of your first pet?" "What was the color of your first car?" You offer answers, and then you must correctly answer the questions when resetting your password or adjusting your account settings. The issue with static KBA is that the average person now shares a great deal about themselves online. Personal accounts like Facebook and Gmail often include basic information normally used to answer static KBA questions. If a hacker can access some of your most basic information, they have a real chance at fooling static KBA.

"Dynamic" KBA is more effective because of the depth and breadth of questions, which reference both current and historical information.[10] Dynamic KBA authentication typically relies on third-party databases with access to public information to provide multiple, sophisticated questions with a range of correct answers.

If static KBA asks about the street you grew up on, dynamic KBA asks "Which of these streets have you NEVER lived on or used as your address?" Instead of asking you about the color of your first car, dynamic KBA will ask you to identify the car models you've owned.

---

10   "The Role of Knowledge Based Authentication (KBA) in Identity Proofing." *LexisNexis*, Dec. 2013, lexisnexis.com/risk/downloads/idm/role-of-knowledge-based-authentication-in-identity-proofing.pdf.

Where static KBA asks questions with single answers that are more easily verifiable, dynamic KBA asks multiple questions with a range of possible answers - everything from all of the above to none at all.

INFRASTRUCTURE BUILT ON TRUST

Security is something that's top of mind for businesses and consumers alike. As more of our information moves online, all parties need assurances that their most sensitive information remains safe.

The annual review from the Identity Theft Resource Center (ITRC) showed 2017 was the worst year for data breaches on record.[11] In 2017, there were 1,579 data breaches (a 44% increase from 2016) that exposed:

- **14.2 million credit cards**
  (+88% from 2016)
- **158 million Social Security numbers**
  (+800% from 2016)
- **179 million total records**
  (+389% from 2016)

---

11   "2017 Annual Data Breach Year-End Review." *Identity Theft Resource Center*, www.idtheftcenter.org/images/breach/2017Breaches/2017AnnualDataBreachYearEndReview.pdf.

The ITRC reported a 23% drop in breaches from 2017 to 2018, but acknowledged a 126% increase in the number of stolen records that contained personally identifiable information (PII).[12] PII is sensitive data used to identify a specific individual – things like your birthday, medical information, or Social Security Number – and lives in dozens of locations online as more companies digitize their systems and processes.

Even if you diligently vet who has access to your most sensitive information, it's nearly impossible to limit who has access to it. Companies often entrust third-party contractors with access to PII to help develop efficiencies or enhance platforms.

Working with a vendor that takes security seriously is vital to the security of consumer information and the health and reputation of a business. Organizations that are SOC 2 compliant are recognized as having a secure business and engineering process from an independent auditor. It's a baseline level of security for some of the world's largest software companies.

Robust data security isn't a nice-to-have; it's a necessity when it comes to PII.

---

12 "2018 End-of-Year Data Breach Report." *Identity Theft Resource Center,* www.idtheftcenter.org/wp-content/uploads/2019/02/ITRC_2018-End-of-Year-Aftermath_FINAL_V2_combinedWEB.pdf

2. Empowering Notaries to Be Their Best

Let's say someone gets through credential analysis and KBA with your identity. All hope is not lost. Perhaps the greatest security feature is the notary themselves.

Intuition is a security feature that can't be built. Notaries may not refuse service based on personal bias or belief, but several states require notaries to refuse service under certain circumstances. This includes when the signer cannot be present, properly identified, or if the notary reasonably believes the signer doesn't understand what they are signing. A good RON vendor will provide the notary with the snapshot of the proof of identity used during credential analysis. Having the photo ID handy – even when not physically present with the signer – allows notaries to act as the final line of defense against fraud.

VIDEO HELPS ENSURE SAFETY

Notaries are responsible for ensuring signers sign documents under their own free will, but little attention is paid to the notary being coerced or pressured into applying their seal.

One NNA study found 30% of notaries have faced pressure to ignore or break the law.[13]

Remote online notarization relies on two-way, audio and video communications that allow remote notaries to conduct business from a safe, secure location, and empowers notaries to fulfill their role as an impartial witness. Transactions are recorded for quality assurance and legal purposes, ensuring procedural consistency and protecting both signers and notaries from allegations of fraud.

Similarly, video can help capture subtle hints of signers requesting notarizations under duress. A notary - remote or otherwise - has no magical power to detect duress, especially duress which occurs subtly and over time - such as family pressure - or duress which occurs outside the room, such as financial pressure or threats.

Remote online notarization offers a clear recording of what occurred and a clear opportunity for the notary to ask the signer key questions, on the record, to confirm that the signer understands what they are signing and are doing so of their own free will.

---

13   Thun, David. "What Every Office Notary Should Know." National Notary Association, 16 Sep. 2015, https://www.nationalnotary.org/notary-bulletin/blog/2015/09/what-every-office-notary-should-know.

3. Providing Access for All

Technology has enhanced almost every aspect of our lives. Two-day shipping dwarfs the speed of sending in an order form from the back of a catalog. Push notifications deliver the news hours - even days - faster than the morning paper.

Neither of these technologies produces an inferior product, and neither does online notarization. Having access to a notary when and where you need one is the apex of access, allowing this vital public service to be available on your terms - not the other way around.

It empowers not only the average person or business, but some of the most underserved and disenfranchised members of our communities. There are people who work 12-hour days to make ends meet that can't go to a bank during normal business hours. There are others with limitations or disabilities for whom accessing a notary is exceedingly difficult and for whom accessing a mobile notary can be a difficult expense.

Digitizing the notary process grants independence. Life's most important moments no longer hinge on proximity or availability.

It's also a boon to the nation's most important economic sectors, which require confidence in the intrinsic trust provided by the notarial seal. These sectors accounted for roughly 37% of the nation's $19.485 trillion gross domestic product (GDP) in 2017:[14,15]

- **Real estate, renting, and leasing**
  3.3% of GDP (approx. $2.59 trillion)
- **State and local government**
  8.7% (approx. $1.7 trillion)
- **Finance and insurance**
  7.6% (approx. $1.48 trillion)
- **Health and social care**
  7.5% (approx. $1.46 trillion)

---

14 "U.S. Gross Domestic Product, 2017." *Federal Reserve Bank of St. Louis*, fred.stlouisfed.org/series/GDP#b.

15 "Value Added by Industry as a Percentage of U.S. Gross Domestic Product, 2017." *Federal Reserve Bank of St. Louis*, fred.stlouisfed.org/release/tables?rid=331&eid=211

CHAPTER 4

Laws and Recognition

Notaries public had an early presence in the New World, dating back to when Rodrigo de Escobedo accompanied Christopher Columbus on his voyage to the Americas in 1492.[16] Thomas Fugill became the first New World notary in 1639,[17] and as commerce picked up between England and its colonies, so too did the value of the notary public.

Over the last 200 years, a number of state laws have shaped a legal framework for interstate acceptance of online notarial acts.

---

16 "Notary History." *National Notary Association*, www.nationalnotary.org/knowledge-center/about-notaries/notary-history.

17 "Notary Public Day." *American Society of Notaries*, www.asnnotaryorg/?form=notarypublicdayis november7.

It's important for you to understand the connection between these laws and how they impact the legality of RON. Here are the documents and legislation that guide the notarial act in the United States.

The Full Faith and Credit Clause

As the United States government began to take shape following the Declaration of Independence, the value of recognizing the official acts of sister states was paramount. The nation's first Constitution was the Articles of Confederation,[18] an agreement among the 13 original states that addressed how to govern the new nation.

The Articles went into effect in 1781 and were limited in scope and power, but they preserved the independence and sovereignty of states - a principle that carries on today.

The Articles also expressly acknowledged the duties of to respect the public acts, records, and judicial proceedings of every other state through a Full Faith and Credit Clause. Article IV of the Articles of Confederation reads:

---

18 "Articles of Confederation: March 1, 1781." *The Avalon Project at Yale Law Lillian Goldman Law Library*, avalon.law.yale.edu/18th_century/artconf.asp.

> *"Full faith and credit shall be given in each of these States to the records, acts, and judicial proceedings of the courts and magistrates of every other State."*

The Articles of Confederation were replaced by the United States Constitution in 1789,[19] which included its own Full Faith and Credit Clause in Article IV, Section 1:

> *"Full faith and credit shall be given in each state to the public acts, records, and judicial proceedings of every other state. And the Congress may by general laws prescribe the manner in which such acts, records, and proceedings shall be proved, and the effect thereof."*

INTERSTATE RECOGNITION

A foundational element of the Full Faith and Credit Clause is the principle of interstate recognition of notarial acts. The authority and validity of a notarized document have been honored in the U.S. for four centuries, even as states grew to adopt their own processes and commission requirements.

---

19 "The Bill of Rights & All Amendments." *The Constitution of the United States*, constitutionus.com/.

The trust tied to a notarized document is critical to both consumers and businesses, across state lines and abroad.

To ensure the free flow of interstate commerce, each state has implemented specific state-level statutes which reinforce and clarify their unconditional recognition and acceptance of each other state's notarial acts. The reason for this long-standing, reciprocal interstate recognition is simple: Americans notarize over a billion documents each year, and those documents are used all over the country.

Notarial acts are "valid" forever, regardless of time or location. That's because reciprocal interstate recognition rests on the idea that notarizations are:

- **Portable**: A duly notarized document is accepted as such essentially anywhere in the United States without further proof of the notary's authority; and
- **Durable**: A duly notarized document retains its value over time.

Notaries regularly perform notarial acts for documents intended to be used in other states, either for in-state residents who have business or property in other states, or for other states' residents who are traveling and need a document notarized for use back home.

Interstate recognition is more than a matter of convenience. It's vital to interstate commerce that states recognize the integrity of the notarial act, even if the legal requirements for the notarial transaction do not sync up across states. Interstate recognition has been repeatedly applied by the Supreme Court and many lower-level courts over the last 150 years.

The Uniform Law Commission

The Uniform Law Commission (ULC),[20] is a nonpartisan, nonprofit association of practicing lawyers, judges, legislators, and legislative staff, and law professors.

For over 125 years, the members of ULC have been appointed by state governments to research, draft, and promote enactment of uniform state laws in areas of state law where uniformity is desirable and practical.

The ULC has been involved for more than a century in two pivotal efforts related to the notarial act: The Commission is committed to ensuring the uniform and conditional interstate recognition of notarial acts, as well as bringing uniformity to state-by-state regulation of the notarial act.

---

20   *The Uniform Law Commission*, www.uniformlaws.org.

As you will see, the ULC has been critical in drafting uniform acknowledgment legislation for notarial acts dating back to its earliest days as an association. This legislation includes:

- **The Uniform Acknowledgments Act** (1892), one of the first four acts passed by the ULC;
- **The Uniform Foreign Acknowledgments Act** (1914), which extended acknowledgments to those taken outside of the United States;
- **The Uniform Acknowledgments Act** (1939), which made the notarial seal self-authenticating, meaning that it is accepted as valid and proper without further evidence of the notary's authority;
- **The Uniform Recognition of Acknowledgments Act** (1968), which extended the self-authenticating recognition to all notarial acts; and
- **The Uniform Law on Notarial Acts** (1982), which retained provisions regarding uniform interstate recognition of notarial acts and provided uniform provisions for regulating notarial acts.

RULONA

The Revised Uniform Law on Notarial Acts (RULONA) was created by the ULC in 2010. This legislation included provisions and infrastructure requirements to perform notarial acts using electronic records and signatures.[21]

RULONA was updated in 2018 to further recognize electronic notarial acts and put them on a par with notarial acts performed on tangible media.[22] Among the new amendments was Section 14A, which authorized notaries public to conduct remote online notarizations through identity-proofing and audio-video communication technologies.

UETA

The Uniform Electronic Transactions Act (UETA)[23] was approved by the ULC during its annual meeting in 1999. UETA gives electronic signatures related to business, commercial, and government transactions the same legal effect as traditional handwritten signatures.

---

21 Memo on the "Revised Uniform Law on Notarial Acts (2018)." *Uniform Law Commission*, my.uniformlaws.org/HigherLogic/System/DownloadDocumentFile.ashx?DocumentFileKey=3bb666b1-5146-9ef2-95c3-cf75e5efb663&forceDialog=0.

22 "Revised Uniform Law on Notarial Acts (2018)." *Uniform Law Commission*, my.uniformlaws.org/HigherLogic/System/DownloadDocumentFile.ashx?DocumentFileKey=c19906b9-b521-4e6c-63d1-30ebf6248e2&forceDialog=0.

23 "Uniform Electronic Transactions Act (1999)." *Uniform Law Commission*, www.uniformlaws.org/HigherLogic/System/DownloadDocumentFile.ashx?DocumentFileKey=dac19487-e89c-0305-53fd-b0da7d68d22f&forceDialog=0.

UETA defines an "electronic signature" as an electronic sound, symbol, or process attached to or logically associated with a record and executed or adopted by a person with the intent to sign the record.

Through 2018, UETA has been adopted by 47 states, the District of Columbia, Puerto Rico, and Guam.[24] Three states have enacted comparable eSignature legislation in lieu of UETA:

- **Washington**: Enacted the Electronic Authentication Act[25] in 1997, the first law of its kind in the United States.
- **Illinois**: Enacted the Electronic Commerce Security Act[26] in 1999.
- **New York**: Enacted the Electronic Signatures and Records Act[27] in 2000.

---

24 "Electronic Transactions Act (1999)." *Uniform Law Commission*, my.uniformlaws.org/committees/community-home?CommunityKey=2c04b76c-2b7d-4399-977e-d5876ba7e034

25 "Electronic Authentication Act." *Washington Secretary of State*, www.sos.wa.gov/ea/ea.aspx

26 "Electronic Commerce Security Act." *Illinois General Assembly*, www.ilga.gov/legislation/ilcs/ilcs3.asp?ActID=89&ChapterID=2.e

27 "Electronic Signatures and Records Act (ESRA)." *Office of Information Technology Services, New York State*, its.ny.gov/electronic-signatures-and-records-act-esra.

E-Sign Act

The Electronic Signatures in Global and National Commerce Act (E-Sign Act)[28] is a legislative complement to UETA.

The E-Sign Act allows electronic records to replace paper documents involved in interstate or foreign commerce that require a written signature with the signer's consent. Complimentary record retention laws went into effect in 2001.

UETA and the E-Sign Act only address business, commercial, and government needs. Neither applies to wills, trusts, or a number of other transactions managed by the courts. Those instances require legislative adoption at the state level.

In 2017, Nevada amended its laws to allow for wills to be electronically signed and remotely notarized. Notarize and Trust & Will partnered to execute the nation's first end-to-end digital will in January 2019.[29]

---

28   "Electronic Signatures in Global and National Commerce Act." *Government Publishing Office*, 30 June 2000, www.govinfo.gov/content/pkg/PLAW-106publ229/pdf/PLAW-106publ229.pdf.

29   "Trust & Will and Notarize Partner to Deliver Nation's First End-to-End Digital Will." *Notarize*, 24 Jan. 2019, www.notarize.com/blog/trust-will-and-notarize-partner-to-deliver-nations-first-end-to-end-digital-will.

URPERA

The Uniform Real Property Electronic Recording Act (URPREA)[30] was created by the ULC in 2004. The legislation authorizes land records officials to begin accepting records in electronic form, storing electronic records, and setting up systems for searching for and retrieving these records. The act equates electronic documents and signatures with original paper documents and manual signatures so that electronic transaction documents may be electronically recorded.

URPERA adoption is not a requirement for electronic recording of documents, but the legislation gives county clerks and recorders an additional measure of certainty about the legal authority to electronically record documents relating to real property land records.

Through 2018, URPERA has been adopted by 31 states, the District of Columbia, and the U.S. Virgin Islands.[31]

---

30 "Uniform Real Property Electronic Recording Act (2004)." *Uniform Law Commission*, www.uniformlaws.org/HigherLogic/System/DownloadDocumentFile.ashx?DocumentFileKey=f1c83e50-1877-c0fa-f72d-d88e06a192d3&forceDialog=0.

31 "Real Property Electronic Recording Act (2004)." *Uniform Law Commission*, my.uniformlaws.org/committees/community-home?CommunityKey=643c99ad-6abf-4046-9da4-0a6367da00cc.

However, URPERA does not require a recording office to accept electronic documents.[32] Each office within a state can make its own determination based on the available technology, needs of the marketplace, and financial resources.

According to the Property Records Industry Association (PRIA), [33] these three fundamental enactments – E-Sign Act, UETA, and URPERA – provide "... a basic legal foundation for notaries to utilize an electronic signature and seal when notarizing an electronic document."

Although each state and recording jurisdiction has final say about adoption, eRecording is now quite common. According to PRIA, as of November 1, 2019, 85% of Americans live in jurisdictions that accept eRecorded documents.

---

32 "Why Your State Should Adopt the Uniform Real Property Electronic Recording Act." *Uniform Law Commission*, my.uniformlaws.org/HigherLogic/System/DownloadDocumentFile.ashx?DocumentFileKey=9e8775d0-7dcf-53f6-623c-d8d7ed028bfe&forceDialog=0.

33 "PRIA Position Statement on Electronic and Remote Notary." *Property Records Industry Association*, www.pria.us/files/resource_library_files/Notary/PRIA Position Statement on Electronic Notary_Rules_FINAL(1).pdf.

CHAPTER 5

State of RON

Today, people living in any state can legally get their documents notarized online. When Virginia Code Section 47.1 went into effect in 2012, it enabled anyone with a Social Security Number to get their documents notarized by a commissioned Virginia electronic notary: anywhere, any time.[34]

However, while the law empowered consumers and businesses nationwide, it only benefited Virginia-based notaries. Notaries are state officials, meaning each state must enact RON legislation before their notaries are able to tap into the online notary market.

---

34 "Title 47.1. Notaries and Out-of-State Commissioners." *Virginia's Legislative Information System*, law.lis.virginia.gov/vacode/title47.1/.

But change is coming fast, as remote online notarization has made remarkable strides nationwide. The number of RON-approved states has more than doubled since the end of 2018 – from 10 total states to 22. Six states now actively support online notaries and nearly every state legislature has submitted a RON bill for consideration.

Here are the RON bills signed as of November 1, 2019.

States That Have Implemented RON Legislation

VIRGINIA

Virginia became the first state to adopt remote online legislation when Governor Bob McDonnell signed House Bill 2318/Senate Bill 827 into law on March 26, 2011. The law went into effect July 1, 2012.

MONTANA

Montana became the second state to adopt remote online legislation when Governor Steve Bullock signed Senate Bill 306 into law on May 4, 2015. The law went into effect October 1, 2015.

Senate Bill 306 was unlike the Virginia bill that came before and the RON bills that followed.

It required signers to personally know the notary or be identified to the notary through a credible witness, and with the exception of notarizations related to proxy marriages, signers needed to be legal residents of Montana.

On April 3, 2019, Governor Bullock signed House Bill 370 to align the state's RON laws with 2017 model legislation from the Mortgage Bankers Association (MBA) and the American Land Title Association (ALTA). The updated laws went into effect October 1, 2019.

TEXAS

Texas became the third state to adopt remote online legislation when Governor Greg Abbott signed House Bill 1217 into law on June 1, 2017. The law went into effect on July 1, 2018.

NEVADA

Nevada became the fourth state to adopt remote online legislation when Governor Brian Sandoval signed Assembly Bill 413 into law on June 9, 2017. The law went into effect on July 1, 2018.

TENNESSEE

Tennessee became the sixth state to adopt remote online legislation when Governor Bill Haslam signed House Bill 1794/Senate Bill 1758 into law on May 15, 2018. The law went into effect on July 1, 2019.

MINNESOTA

Minnesota became the seventh state to adopt remote online legislation when Governor Mark Dayton signed Senate File 893 into law on May 20, 2018. The law went into effect on January 1, 2019.

States That Have Passed RON Legislation

INDIANA

Indiana became the fifth state to adopt RON legislation when Governor Eric Holcomb signed Senate Bill 372 into law on March 13, 2018.

The law was originally scheduled to go into effect on July 1, 2019. Governor Holcomb later signed House Bill 1487, which moved the effective date to either July 1, 2020, or when the Secretary of State adopts its rules on RON – whichever comes first.

VERMONT

Vermont became the eighth state to adopt RON legislation when Governor Phil Scott signed House Bill 526 into law on May 22, 2018. The law went into effect on July 1, 2019.

MICHIGAN

Michigan became the ninth state to adopt RON legislation when Governor Rick Snyder signed House Bill 5811 into law on June 26, 2018. The law went into effect on September 26, 2018. Governor Snyder and the Michigan legislature later amended HB5811 with Senate Bill 0664.

OHIO

Ohio became the 10th state to pass RON legislation when Governor John Kasich signed Senate Bill 263 into law on December 19, 2018. The law went into effect on September 19, 2019.

NORTH DAKOTA

North Dakota became the 11th state to pass RON legislation when Governor Doug Burgum signed House Bill 1110 into law on March 8, 2019. The law went into effect on August 1, 2019.

SOUTH DAKOTA

South Dakota became the 12th state to pass RON legislation when Governor Kristi Noem signed House Bill 1272 into law on March 18, 2019. The law went into effect on July 1, 2019.

IDAHO

Idaho became the 13th state to pass RON legislation when Governor Brad Little signed Senate Bill 1111 into law on March 22, 2019. The law is scheduled to go into effect on January 1, 2020.

KENTUCKY

Kentucky became the 14th state to pass RON legislation when Governor Matt Bevin signed Senate Bill 114 into law on March 25, 2019. The law is scheduled to go into effect on January 1, 2020.

UTAH

Utah became the 15th state to pass RON legislation when Governor Gary Herbert signed House Bill 52 into law on March 25, 2019. The law went into effect November 1, 2019.

ARIZONA

Arizona became the 16th state to pass RON legislation when Governor Doug Ducey signed Senate Bill 1030 into law on April 10, 2019. The law is scheduled to go into effect on June 30, 2020.

WASHINGTON

Washington became the 17th state to pass RON legislation when Governor Jay Inslee signed Senate Bill 5641 into law on April 26, 2019. The law is scheduled to go into effect on October 1, 2020.

IOWA

Iowa became the 18th state to pass RON legislation when Governor Kim Reynolds signed Senate File 475 into law on April 29, 2019. The law is scheduled to go into effect on July 1, 2020.

OKLAHOMA

Oklahoma became the 19th state to pass RON legislation when Governor Kevin Stitt signed Senate Bill 915 into law on May 9, 2019. The law is scheduled to go into effect on January 1, 2020.

MARYLAND

Maryland became the 20th state to pass RON legislation when Governor Larry Hogan signed Senate Bill 678 into law on May 13, 2019. The law is scheduled to go into effect on October 1, 2020.

NEBRASKA

Nebraska became the 21st state to pass RON legislation when Governor Pete Ricketts signed Legislative Bill 186 into law on May 30, 2019. The law is scheduled to go into effect on July 1, 2020.

FLORIDA

Florida became the 22nd state to pass RON legislation when Governor Ron DeSantis signed House Bill 409 into law on June 7, 2019. The law is scheduled to go into effect on January 1, 2020.

Exceptions

Despite centuries of universal interstate recognition, Iowa legislators took the unprecedented step of expressly conditioning its acceptance of out-of-state notarizations with a 2012 enactment of Iowa Code Chapter 9B.[35] This represented a departure from the longstanding, nationwide network of unconditional recognition and acceptance of other states' notarial acts.

The updated laws require notarial acts to be performed in conformance with the law of Iowa as a qualification for recognition in Iowa.[36] As such, documents intended for use in Iowa may not be remotely notarized.

However, this will not be the case much longer. Iowa Governor Kim Reynolds signed Senate File 475 into law on April 29, 2019, which will enable Iowa notaries to use remote notarization tools and remove the outlier provisions in Chapter 9B, allowing Iowa to rejoin the other 49 states in recognizing notarial acts from other states.

The law is scheduled to go into effect on July 1, 2020.

---

35 "The Iowa Legislature." *Iowa Code: Chapter 9B*, www.legis.iowa.gov/docs/code//9B.pdf.

36 "The Model Electronic Notarization Act." *National Notary Association*, Jan. 2017, www.nationalnotary.org/filelibrary/nna/reference-library/model-enotarization-act.pdf.

CHAPTER 6

Milestones and Model Legislation

Virginia's RON bill required additional guidance from some of the nation's largest organizations and trade associations. As a result, there have been a number of critical policies and model legislation established that have shaped the scope and impact of RON.

Here are some of the most important.

Model Electronic Notarization Act

The Model Electronic Notarization Act (MENA)[37] of 2017 is a comprehensive standard and guide for public officials who are establishing rules to govern the notarization of electronic records. MENA is the latest NNA model act that weaves best practices for reliable authenticity and fraud deterrence with the high ethical norms expected of a notary public.

MENA is a complement to the Model Notarial Act (MNA), which was first introduced in 1973 and was updated for the fourth time in 2010.[38] The 2010 MNA expanded and refined paper-based notarial provisions and dramatically enhanced the electronic provisions to reflect the evolving demands of technology, business, and government.

NNA's model notarization acts have guided legislators and notary-regulating officials for nearly five decades. Some jurisdictions have adopted these model acts in their entirety, while others have used key components to modernize their notarial laws.

---

37 "The Model Electronic Notarization Act." *National Notary Association*, Jan. 2017, www.nationalnotary.org/filelibrary/nna/reference-library/model-enotarization-act.pdf.

38 "The Model Notary Act." *National Notary Association*, 1 Jan. 2010, www.nationalnotary.org/file%20library/nna/reference-library/2010_model_notary_act.pdf.

The First Fully Digital Mortgage

If there was one form of notarization that was considered nearly untouchable, it was the home closing. Electronic mortgages had been around for years, but convenience and efficiency ended at the closing table. There was always the stipulation that closing documents either needed to be electronically notarized or "wet-signed," meaning pen to paper.

But RON changed everything by empowering the future of home buying: the fully digital mortgage.

In July 2017, an Illinois couple bought a home in Texas using a Texas title company (Stewart Title), a Michigan lender (United Wholesale Mortgage), and a Virginia notary (Notarize).[39] The buyers completed their closing online in 30 minutes, saving thousands of dollars in travel, hundreds of sheets of paper, and days in shipping.

There have been thousands of online mortgage closings since then,[40] proving there is a place in the home buying process for a seamless, end-to-end digital experience.

---

39   Friedman, Robyn A. "Mortgage Closings Just Took a Big Step Into the Digital Age." *The Wall Street Journal*, 9 Aug. 2017, www.wsj.com/articles/mortgage-closings-just-took-a-big-step-into-the-digital-age-1502287181.

40   "Lessons Learned in Closing Over 1,000 Mortgage Transactions Online." *Notarize*, 10 Jan. 2019, www.notarize.com/blog/lessons-learned-closing-one-thousand-mortgage-transactions-online.

MBA/ALTA Model Legislation

In December of 2017, the Mortgage Bankers Association (MBA) and the American Land Title Association (ALTA) released a collaboratively-drafted version of model legislation for state adoption of RON in 2018.[41] The model legislation would create legal certainty across the country from a uniform and consistent framework that is based on a common set of core principles and enables the creation of a fully electronic mortgage experience by MBA and ALTA member companies.

MBA and ALTA drew inspiration for the model legislation from Texas House Bill 1217, which was fine-tuned with input from legislators and industry leaders.[42] On more than one occasion, MBA and ALTA have cited HB 1217 as being well thought out, having adopted and refined language from the Texas text to make RON more suitable in a multistate environment.[43]

[41] "Mortgage Bankers Association – American Land Title Association Model Legislation for Remote Online Notarization." *American Land Title Association*, 19 Dec. 2017, www.alta.org/file.cfm?name=MBA-and-ALTA-Model-Act-FINAL.

[42] *Letter to the Honorable Tan Parker of the Texas House of Representatives*, 1 May 2017, go.notarize.com/hubfs/Texas-Remote-Notary-Support-Letter.pdf.

[43] "Mortgage Bankers Association – American Land Title Association Memo on the Model Legislation for Remote Online Notarization." *American Land Title Association*, 19 Dec. 2017, www.alta.org/file.cfm?name=MBA-ALTA-Memo-on-Model-Bill-Final.

Texas' rules were emulated in Nevada Assembly Bill 413.

MBA is the national association representing the real estate finance industry, an industry that employs more than 280,000 people in virtually every community in the country. Headquartered in Washington, D.C., the association works to ensure the continued strength of the nation's residential and commercial real estate markets; to expand homeownership and extend access to affordable housing to all Americans.

Founded in 1907 and headquartered in Washington, D.C., ALTA is the national trade association and voice of more than 6,000 title insurance agents, abstracters, and underwriters. ALTA Members search, review and insure land titles to protect homebuyers and mortgage lenders who invest in real estate. ALTA is represented by an Active ALTA Member in every county in the United States.

National Association of Secretaries of State

Announced in April 2016, the National Association of Secretaries of State (NASS) developed a Remote Electronic Notarization Task Force to help states understand the issues and policies surrounding RON.

In February 2018, NASS and its members approved a Revised National Electronic Notarization Standards,[44] including RON definitions, standards, and requirements.

NASS previously adopted the National Electronic Notarization Standards in 2006.[45] The standards, at the time, allowed for documents to be signed electronically on a tablet or computer, but much like traditional notarization laws, still required physical in-person appearance to verify identity. This restriction is what made Virginia's 2011 law, in part, so significant.

NASS is the nation's oldest, nonpartisan professional organization for public officials. Founded in 1904, NASS serves as a medium for the exchange of information between states and fosters cooperation in the development of public policy.

---

44 "NASS Support for the Revised National Electronic Notarization Standards." *National Association of Secretaries of State*, 19 Feb. 2018, www.nass.org/sites/default/files/resolutions/2018-02/nass-support-revised-enotarization-standards-winter18_0.pdf.

45 "NASS Resolution Reaffirming Support for the National Electronic Notarization Standards." *National Association of Secretaries of State*, 17 July 2016, www.nass.org/sites/default/files/resolutions/2016/resolution-business-services-Enotary-standards-final-summer2016.pdf.

United States Department of the Treasury

In July 2018, the U.S. Department of the Treasury released *A Financial System That Creates Economic Opportunities: Nonbank Financials, Fintech, and Innovation*.[46] This 223-page report highlighted areas of stagnation and opportunity within the American financial system and offered recommendations for businesses, policymakers, and government officials to help jumpstart economic growth.

One of the key opportunities identified within the lending and servicing industries was electronic closings and recordings.

The report cited a 2015 eClosing pilot by the Consumer Financial Protection Bureau (CFPB) which found RON adoption and implementation was a key remaining impediment to the digital mortgage process and offered additional borrower satisfaction and convenienceover traditional paper closings.[47]

---

[46] "A Financial System That Creates Economic Opportunities Nonbank Financials, Fintech, and Innovation." *Department of the Treasury*, July 2018, home.treasury.gov/sites/default/files/2018-07/A-Financial-System-that-Creates-Economic-Opportunities---Nonbank-Financi....pdf.

[47] "Leveraging Technology to Empower Mortgage Consumers at Closing: Learnings From the EClosing Pilot." *Consumer Financial Protection Bureau*, Aug. 2015, files.consumerfinance.gov/f/201508_cfpb_leveraging-technology-to-empower-mortgage-consumers-at-closing.pdf.

It also identified a lack of broad statutory acceptance and uneven standards nationwide as a reason for slow adoption.

The Treasury made four RON-specific recommendations:

- That states yet to authorize electronic and remote notarizations pursue legislation and the interstate recognition of remotely notarized documents.
- That states align laws and regulations to further standardize notarization practices.
- That Congress should consider legislation to provide a minimum uniform national standard for electronic and remote online notarizations.
- That recording jurisdictions yet to recognize and accept electronic records adopt the necessary technologies to process and record these documents and to pursue digitization of existing property records.

The National Association of REALTORS®

At the 2018 REALTORS® Conference and Expo, the National Association of REALTORS® (NAR) approved a policy that supports the adoption of RON standards, laws, and regulations.[48]

---

48 "NAR Board Supports New Notary Technologies." *National*

As part of this effort, NAR will work with interested groups and federal agencies to actively facilitate remote notarization adoption across the mortgage ecosystem. The announcement followed a February 2018 letter from NAR President Elizabeth Mendenhall to the National Association of Secretaries of State, which cited flexibility and greater integrity through enhanced security as benefits of widespread RON adoption.[49]

NAR is the nation's largest trade association, representing 1.3 million members through institutes, societies, and councils that touch all aspects of the residential and commercial real estate industries. Members belong to one or more of approximately 1,200 local associations/boards and 54 state and territory associations of REALTORS®.

MISMO Remote Notarization Technology Standards

The Mortgage Industry Standards Maintenance Organization (MISMO) is the mortgage industry's standards

---

Association of REALTORS®, 5 Nov. 2018, magazine.realtor/daily-news/2018/11/05/nar-board-supports-new-notary-technologies.

49 "Letter to Leslie Reynolds, Executive Director of the National Association of Secretaries of State." *National Association of REALTORS®*, 16 Feb. 2018, www.narfocus.com/billdatabase/clientfiles/172/3/3105.pdf.

development body. The organization is responsible for developing a common data language for exchanging information for the residential finance industry.

In the summer of 2019, MISMO released its long-awaited RON standards for public comment,[50] the culmination of a two-year effort by the Remote Online Notarization Development Workgroup to create industry standards and other collateral that would enable electronic and online notaries to facilitate real estate transactions.

The workgroup worked with government officials, industry insiders, and others to develop standards for online notarization that will enable mortgage participants to quickly adopt new practices to facilitate the use of online notaries to meet consumer demand.

MISMO's RON standards support the model legislation previously released by the Mortgage Bankers Association and the American Land Title Association. MISMO also noted that some states relied on draft versions of the MISMO RON standards when developing their RON legislation.

MISMO released its final standards on September 9, 2019.

---

50 "MISMO Approves New Online Notarization Standards." *Mortgage Industry Standards Maintenance Organization*, http://www.mismo.org/news-and-events/all-news/mismo-approves-new-online-notarization-standards-

Conclusion

Remote online notarizations allow people to buy a home in Texas while they're visiting family in Massachusetts, or to take the trip of a lifetime with young children. It allows someone overseas to recover a stolen passport in minutes when it may take days or weeks through the U.S. Embassy.

As your state gets ready to adopt this technology, or begins enforcing laws in favor of it, here's how you can prepare.

Read the Bill

When your governor signs the RON bill into law, it includes a framework about how RON will operate in your state.

Some of these rules are high-level explanations about the business being conducted, whereas others might be nuanced explanations for how you should conduct yourself as an online notary.

Stay In the Know

Businesses and potential notaries alike should review the bill for key dates and definitions. The final rules for RON often lie with your state legislature, who will release a final set of regulations in the weeks and months ahead of the enforcement date. State officials will also release information about application acceptance dates, classes, exams - anything related to getting your online notary certification off the ground.

Rally Your Team

In order for RON to be impactful, you need to get buy-in from each stakeholder in your organization. The process of using technology to notarize documents from anywhere demands a highly collaborative and communicative infrastructure. When everyone supports each other, that's when you can truly deliver a solution to serve your state.

Frequently Asked Questions

Q: Is remote online notarization legal?
A: As of November 1, 2019, 22 states have passed laws that enable their notaries to conduct remote notarizations for anyone with a Social Security Number – regardless of their location. Every state has its own legal authority for the recognition and acceptance of out-of-state notarizations. Only Iowa does not accept remotely notarized documents – but this will change July 1, 2020.

Q: Is this technology available in my state?
A: States have a longstanding regime of interstate recognition statutes that recognize and accept notarizations from other states.

For this reason, an online notary public in a state which has authorized its notaries to use RON tools may legally notarize your documents and you may generally use them in other states as you would a paper-notarized document.

While RON is legal, not everyone accepts electronic documents. Always check with your intended recipient to confirm they accept electronically signed and notarized documents.

Q: What documents can be remotely notarized?
A: Federal and state laws allow for many types of documents to be electronically signed. There are exceptions for a few categories of documents, and some states, public agencies, and court systems impose specific additional requirements, limitations, and conditions for accepting electronically-signed documents. It's always a great idea to check with your intended recipient to confirm they accept these notarized documents.

Q: Is this technology replacing notaries?
A: Remote online notarization does many wonderful things for the role of notary public. Identities are more easily verifiable, the transaction is more secure, and a good vendor will retain a recording of the session should the validity of the transaction come into question.

This also makes notarization an attractive job in the "gig" economy. There's no storefront or car needed to help people with the most important transactions of their lives. Notaries, too, can do business from a safe, comfortable environment.

Q: Are RON companies just notary farms?
A: Speed and efficiency should not be seen as a detriment to quality and care. Amazon's two-day shipping dwarfs the speed of sending in an order form from the back of a catalog. Push notifications deliver the news hours - sometimes days - faster than the morning paper. Neither technology produces an inferior product.

The same is true for RON, which maximizes efficiencies within and around the notarial act. Signers can connect with a notary in a fraction of the time required to travel to an office park or wait on a mobile notary. Meeting customer needs sooner allows remote notaries to do more business.

But it's not just about the customer experience. Remote online notarization platforms empower notaries with the ability to serve their profession and engage with their customers on their own time. Notaries may choose to work full-time in a traditional employment model or part-time from the comfort of their home.

Q: Where can I learn more?
A: Visit notarize.com for the latest information about RON.

Key Terms

Electronic: Relating to technology having electrical, digital, magnetic, wireless, optical, electromagnetic, or similar capabilities.

Electronic notarization: Documents are notarized in an electronic form where the signer uses an electronic signature but physically appears before the notary.

Electronic notary public: A public official commissioned to certify contracts, deeds, and other documents. Electronic notaries may only perform notarizations online if their state has adopted RON legislation. States that have only in-person electronic notarization laws also call their notaries electronic notaries.

Electronic Signature or **e-Signature** or **eSignature**: An electronic sound, symbol, or process, attached to or logically associated with a contract or other record and executed or adopted by a person with the intent to sign the record.

Notary public: A public official commissioned to certify contracts, deeds, and other documents through an in-person engagement with a signer.

Remote online notarization: Documents are notarized in an electronic form where the signer uses an electronic signature and appears before the notary using online audio-video technology.

Bibliography

"2017 Data Breach Year-End Review." *Identity Theft Resource Center*, idtheftcenter.org/imagesbreach/2017 Breaches/2017 AnnualDataBreachYearEndReview.pdf.

"2018 End-of-Year Data Breach Report." *Identity Theft Resource Center*, www.idtheftcenter.org/wp-content/uploads/2019/02/ITRC_ 2018-End-of-Year-Aftermath_ FINAL_V2_combinedWEB.pdf.

The American Society of Questioned Document Examiners, www.asqde.org/.

"Articles of Confederation: March 1, 1781." *The Avalon*

Project at Yale Law Lillian Goldman Law Library, avalon.law.yale.edu/18th_century/ artconf.asp.

"The Bill of Rights & All Amendments." *The Constitution of the United States*, constitutionus.com/.

"Electronic Authentication Act." *Washington Secretary of State*, www.sos.wa.gov/ea/ea.aspx.

"Electronic Commerce Security Act." *Illinois General Assembly*, www.ilga.gov/legislation/ilcs/ilcs3.asp?ActID=89&ChapterID=2.e.

"Electronic Signatures and Records Act (ESRA)." *Office of Information Technology Services, New York State*, its.ny.gov/electronic-signatures- and-records-act-esra.

"Electronic Signatures in Global and National Commerce Act." *Government Publishing Office*, 30 June 2000, www.govinfo.gov/ content/pkg/PLAW-106publ229/pdf/PLAW-106publ229.pdf.

"Electronic Transactions Act (1999)." *Uniform Law Commission*, my.uniformlaws.org/committees/community-home?Community Key=2c04b76c-2b7d-4399-977e-d5876ba7e034.

"A Financial System That Creates Economic Opportunities Nonbank Financials, Fintech, and Innovation." *United*

States Department of the Treasury, July 2018, https://home.treasury.gov

Fleming, Mark. "Will Fintech Adoption Among Real Estate Professionals Accelerate in 2019?" *First American*, 27 Nov. 2018, blog.firstam.com/economics/will-fintech-adoption-among-real-estate- professionals-accelerate-in-2019.

Friedman, Robyn A. "Mortgage Closings Just Took a Big Step Into the Digital Age." *The Wall Street Journal*, 9 Aug. 2017, www.wsj.com/articles/mortgage-closings-just-took-a-big-step-into-the- digital-age-1502287181.

"The Iowa Legislature." *Iowa Code: Chapter 9B*, www.legis.iowa.gov/ docs/code//9B.pdf.

"Lessons Learned in Closing Over 1,000 Mortgage Transactions Online." *Notarize*, 10 Jan. 2019, www.notarize.com/blog/lessons-learned- closing-one-thousand-mortgage-transactions-online.

Letter to the Honorable Tan Parker of the Texas House of Representatives, 1 May 2017, go.notarize.com/hubfs/Texas-Remote- Notary-Support-Letter.pdf.

Letter to Leslie Reynolds, Executive Director of the National Association of Secretaries of State, from the National Association of REALTORS®, 16 Feb. 2018, www.narfocus.com/billdatabase/clientfiles/172/3/ 3105.pdf.

"Leveraging Technology to Empower Mortgage Consumers at Closing: Learnings from the eClosing Pilot." *Consumer Financial Protection Bureau*, Aug. 2015, files.consumer finance.gov/f/201508_cfpb_ leveraging-technology-to-empower-mortgage-consumers-at-closing.pdf.

Lewis, Michael. "Notaries Post Mixed Results In Face-Matching Research Survey." *National Notary Association*, 12 Nov. 2015, www.nationalnotary.org/notary-bulletin/blog/2015/11/face-matching- research-results.

Lewis, Michael. "The Notary Challenge: Matching Faces To ID Harder Than You Think." *National Notary Association*, 25 Sept. 2014, www.nationalnotary.org/notary-bulletin/blog/2014/09/matching- faces-to-id-harder.

Memo on the "Revised Uniform Law on Notarial Acts (2018)." *Uniform Law Commission*, my.uniformlaws.org/

"The Model Electronic Notarization Act." *National Notary Association*, www.nationalnotary.org/File%20Library/NNA/Reference- Library/Model-eNotarization-Act.pdf.

"The Model Notary Act." *National Notary Association*, 1 Jan. 2010, www.nationalnotary.org/file%20library/nna/reference-library/2010_ model_notary_act.pdf.

"MBA/ALTA Model Legislation for Remote Online Notarization." *American Land Title Association,* 19 Dec. 2017, www.alta.org/file.cfm?name=MBA-and- ALTA-Model-Act-FINAL.

"NAR Board Supports New Notary Technologies." *National Association of REALTORS®,* 5 Nov. 2018, magazine.realtor/daily-news/2018/11/ 05/nar-board-supports-new-notary-technologies.

"NASS Resolution Reaffirming Support for the National Electronic Notarization Standards." *National Association of Secretaries of State,* 17 July 2016, www.nass.org/sites/default/files/resolutions/2016/ resolution-business-services-enotary-standards-final-summer2016.pdf.

"NASS Support for the Revised National Electronic Notarization Standards." *National Association of Secretaries of State,* 19 Feb. 2018, www.nass.org/sites/default/files/resolutions/2018-02/nass-support- revised-enotarization-standards-winter18_0.pdf.

National Notary Association, www.nationalnotary.org/.

"Notary History." *National Notary Association,* nationalnotary.org/knowledge-center/about-notaries/

notary-history.

"Notary Public Day." *American Society of Notaries*, www. asnnotary. org/?form=notarypublicdayisnovember7.

Papesh, Megan H. "Photo ID verification remains challenging despite years of practice" *Cognitive Research: Principles and Implications*, vol. 3 19. 27 Jun. 2018.

"PRIA Position Statement on Electronic and Remote Notary." *Property Records Industry Association*, www. pria.us/files/resource_library_ files/Notary/PRIA Position Statement on Electronic Notary_Rules_ FINAL(1).pdf.

"Real Property Electronic Recording Act (2004)." *Uniform Law Commission*, my.uniformlaws.org/committees/community- home?CommunityKey=643c99ad-6abf-4046-9da4-0a6367da00cc.

"Remote Online Notarization Development Workgroup." *Mortgage Industry Standards Maintenance Organization*, www.mismo.org/get- started/participate-in-a-mismo-workgroup/remote-online-notarization- dwg.

"Revised Uniform Law on Notarial Acts (2018)." *Uniform Law Commission*, my.uniformlaws.org/

"The Role of Knowledge Based Authentication (KBA)

in Identity Proofing." *LexisNexis*, Dec. 2013, lexisnexis.com/risk/downloads/ idm/role-of-knowledge-based-authentication-in-identity-proofing.pdf.

Stein, Elbridge W., et al. "Ball-Point Pens: Use for Signing Legal Documents Considered." *American Bar Association Journal*, vol. 34, no. 5, 1948, pp. 373–378.

Thun, David. "What Every Office Notary Should Know." *National Notary Association*, 16 Sep. 2015, https://www.nationalnotary.org/notary-bulletin/blog/2015/09/what-every-office-notary-should-know.

"Title 47.1. Notaries and Out-of-State Commissioners." *Virginia's Legislative Information System*, law.lis.virginia.gov/vacode/title47.1/.

"Trust & Will and Notarize Partner to Deliver Nation's First End-to-End Digital Will." *Notarize*, 24 Jan. 2019, www.notarize.com/blog/trust- will-and-notarize-partner-to-deliver-nations-first-end-to-end-digital- will.

"U.S. Gross Domestic Product, 2017." *Federal Reserve Bank of St. Louis*, fred.stlouisfed.org/series/GDP#b.

"Uniform Electronic Transactions Act (1999)." *Uniform Law Commission*, www.uniformlaws.org/
The Uniform Law Commission, www.uniformlaws.org.

"Uniform Real Property Electronic Recording Act (2004)." *Uniform Law Commission*, www.uniformlaws.org/

"Value Added by Industry as a Percentage of U.S. Gross Domestic Product, 2017." *Federal Reserve Bank of St. Louis*, fred.stlouisfed.org/ release/tables?rid=331&eid=211.

"The Virginia Electronic Notarization Assurance Standard." *Secretary of the Commonwealth of Virginia*, 21 Jan. 2013, www.commonwealth. virginia.gov/media/governorvirginiagov/secretary-of-the- commonwealth/pdf/VAe-NotarizationStandard2013Version10.pdf.

"Why Your State Should Adopt the Uniform Real Property Electronic Recording Act." *Uniform Law Commission*, my.uniformlaws.org

Notarize is the first platform to empower thousands of people each day to sign and notarize documents online. From adopting a child to buying a home, Notarize builds trusted products and services that support life's most important moments.

For more information, visit notarize.com.

www.ingramcontent.com/pod-product-compliance
Lightning Source LLC
Chambersburg PA
CBHW030954240526
45463CB00016B/2547